He was still young enough to know that the heart's memory eliminates the bad and magnifies the good, and that thanks to this artifice we manage to endure the burden of the past.

GABRIEL GARCÍA MÁRQUEZ

STUBBORN

Poems by Roland Flint

UNIVERSITY OF ILLINOIS PRESS
Urbana and Chicago

To my sisters and brothers,
and in memory of my son and mother

© 1990 by Roland Flint
Manufactured in the United States of America
P 5 4 3

This book is printed on acid-free paper.

Library of Congress Cataloging-in-Publication Data

Flint, Roland.
    Stubborn : poems / by Roland Flint.
        p.   cm.
    ISBN 0-252-06132-2 (alk. paper)
    I. Title.
PS3556.L56S76   1990
811'.54—dc20   89-20549
                                              CIP

Acknowledgments

Some of these poems first appeared in literary magazines and journals, as follows: "Nocturne" and "Measure for Elizabeth" appeared in the *Denver Quarterly;* "Anniversaries" and "Late September, Early Morning" in *Milkweed Chronicle;* "Cinema" in *New Letters;* "Park River Valentines" appeared in the *New Virginia Review;* "What I Have Tried to Say to You" and "For Gabriel's Hands" in *Prairie Schooner;* "Pamela, on February 8, 1982" in *Tendril;* "Bang!" appeared (as "Chop") in *Tri-Quarterly.*

"Jim" and "A Letter Home" first appeared in *From Mt. San Angelo,* an anthology from the Virginia Center for the Creative Arts; both later appeared in *TriQuarterly.*

The following poems first appeared in *Sicily,* a chapbook from North Carolina Wesleyan College Press: "Are You in Town Too?" "Love Which Alters," "Park River, North Dakota: 1939," "Battle of the Bulge, 1944," "What Forgiveness," "Snug Harbor, New Orleans," and "Sicily." The writer wishes to acknowledge that the image (and idea) in the last lines of "What Forgiveness" he has taken, with little change, from Saul Bellow's *Mr. Sammler's Planet.*

The following poems first appeared in souvenir editions from North Carolina Wesleyan College Press: "A Spotted Cat in Indonesia" (which will soon appear in *Shenandoah*), "Gift" (as "The Gift"), "Still" (which later appeared in *The Cooke Book: A Seasoning of Poets*), "Stubborn" (which later appeared in the *New Virginia Review*), and "Black Sea, Mother and Son" (which later appeared in *TriQuarterly*).

The author wishes to acknowledge support from the National Endowment for the Arts and from the Maryland State Arts Council, and to express gratitude for the hospitality of the following artists' colonies: Yaddo, MacDowell, and the Virginia Center for the Creative Arts, during residencies at which he wrote some of these poems.

The National Poetry Series

The National Poetry Series was established in 1978 to publish five collections of poetry annually through five participating publishers—E. P. Dutton, Persea Books, Atlantic Monthly Press, Copper Canyon Press, and the University of Illinois Press. The manuscripts are selected by five poets of national reputation. Publication is funded by the Copernicus Society of America, James A. Michener, Edward J. Piszek, and The Lannan Foundation.

1989

The Brother's Country by Tom Andrews
Selected by Charles Wright. Persea Books

Terra Firma by Thomas Centolella
Selected by Denise Levertov. Copper Canyon Press.

Blessings in Disguise by David Clewell
Selected by Quincy Troupe. E. P. Dutton

Stubborn by Roland Flint
Selected by Dave Smith. University of Illinois Press

Artist and Model by Carol Snow
Selected by Robert Hass. Atlantic Monthly Press

Contents

Home

A Letter Home

Mother I'm sure you remember
when I almost hanged myself in the kitchen?
I was fourteen and had just inherited
milking the cows from Allen
whose time doing chores must have ended
when he graduated from high school.
I wasn't mad about doing them.

Anyway, that night I came in from milking,
after feeding hogs, calves, chickens,
and hung myself. Of course you remember.
In the kitchen by the sink
we had that towel—I haven't seen one since—
a single cotton loop,
four feet long, a foot wide,
hanging from a wooden spool or dowel
affixed to the wall.
The lower end must have been
not quite sink-high: I hung from that.

You came from your radio program
to find me, still wearing my mackinaw,
chore-cap and buckle overshoes.
My feet were behind me, on the scatter rug.
I was face down and slung forward,
the towel was under my chin,
my hands just off the floor,
dead still.

You said as soon as you got me free
I started to breathe and get my color.
Thank God I came in when I did thank God,
you cried and cried, rocking
my head and shoulders to you,
sitting on the floor. It may have been
the last time you held me so.

When I could talk I told you
that I remembered slipping on the rug and falling,
that I must have hit my head on something
and, throat-first, fallen into that loop.

Mother, this month I'm going to be forty-nine,
I've never told you the truth about that night,
and I want to tell you now.
I don't think I meant to die,
but I did hang myself—not quite by accident:
I came in, set the milk pail down, and,
perfectly idly, deliberate and purposeless,
I put the towel under my chin,
stretched out, keeping my overshoes on the rug,
lowered my body, then my hands,
and swung there, as I'd done before—often.
Dreaming, I suppose, but about what?
I don't know anymore, maybe I never knew.
The last thing I remember was
a kind of tingling all over
and a sound—like time. Maybe
I was trying to dream about hanging myself,
how it would be, or acting out a movie fantasy
of my execution by the lynch-mob—
maybe it was something like that—
but it's possible I was thinking of nothing.

What a nightmare I was to you—
I might have died many times,
from carelessness or experimenting:
I almost drowned when I was seven.
It was just luck I didn't fall twenty-five feet
to the concrete floor of the potato warehouse.
I was sideswiped twice by cars, hit by a truck.
All from recklessness, all my fault.
When I was fifteen, I dove
from a tree and knocked myself out

on a rock in the river's bottom.
I played on the tops of moving freight cars.
Dove into snowbanks from the roof of a store.
Three times, once driving,
I was in cars or trucks that rolled over.
And once, with a bellyful of beer
I tried to chugalug a (stolen) fifth of
Seagram's whiskey. All this before I was nineteen.
And before I became as I have now become
very careful and willing to live,
as you are doing, for a long time.

I have been brooding on all those we know
who have been killed in a few seconds' surprise.
And about altering this one incident for you—
if not quite removing it
from that list you must have made by now
of the merciless tricks freak accidents can pull.
We don't have to name our dead, do we?

I'm sorry I lied. I must have thought
I'd catch hell. I know it gave you nightmares.
And I've had mine: when Elizabeth was two
she was standing on the car seat beside me,
I was driving, we were taking a big curve,
and the passenger door swung open.

She did not quite fall,
but I've dreamed it over, waking and sleeping,
ever since—and she's almost nineteen now.
I'm also sorry I waited
thirty-five years to tell you.
I hope it makes a difference to you,
it does to me: it reminds me to say
Thank God you came in when you did,
mother, for the life you gave,
what it's been, what it will be.

For Gabriel's Hands

Fisted, both of them:
thirty seconds after the caesarean
says the note with the picture—
his closed eyes squint
fiercely keeping the dark,
blood on his head, the cilial hair,
and on the left shoulder a chakra of white.
Blood on the small wide fists
squared up to the camera
making them even bigger
than the big baby hands
they unmistakably are—
a cub's predicting the full growth,
which pleases his father.
Someone's holding him up
toward the camera,
the umbilical not yet cut and
dandling still into his mother, uncoiled,
like a phone cord but four times thicker—
in its dull slick dark blue
it's handsome, a surprise to me
if not to his father (a doctor)
who took the picture.
It's a sad first reflex, Gabriel,
but a true one, to make both fists
to the new cold world. After
that bad if timely cutting
of your emergence why should you
open a hand to shake with it?
When mostly you will find apt
your blood-clabbered entering.
There are some exceptions
as I hope my hand closing
to its old light fist around a pen,
this will begin to be.

Are You in Town Too?

Grandma Rose saved quarters
in the cylindrical glass tubes
from which she had removed tablets
for indigestion. I guess
she saved them to give us, or
to buy the gifts with which she came.
Maybe emptying and filling them so
relieved her fatal stomach for a while.
Though they had irresistible heft, the quarters,
banked like that, I forget if I took any,
but she was trusting—and I did steal
Indian-head pennies from my mother's collection:
fifteen at a time, for chocolate Half Pint Sundaes
at the Luxury Ice Cream Store and Creamery,
where that Norwegian farmer asked another,
"Are you in town today, too, then?" "No,"
said the other, "I just come in with the cream."
As if to be in town you had to be in town
to *be* there, rather like being "at home,"
at a certain time, or "receiving," a sense
of occasion, as had Grandmother Rose,
whenever she came to us,
the visiting grandmother come:
to give us gifts, to be neatly dressed in black,
her big purse smelling inside of lilac,
Alka Seltzer, the leathery cloth and glass,
and the silver-warm smell of quarters.

Love Which Alters

Love is not love
Which alters when it alteration finds
Or bends with the remover to remove.

A new friend writes, and, closing, says
"All is well here, though some things
have changed. Inevitable."
She doesn't know you well enough
to say what things, just signs off so,
sending you worry for her marriage,
for two small children in her house,
where, only a year and a half ago,
unmistakably, there was love.
And you hope this is not among the changed.

But it does alter and is not fixed,
as nearly everything says.
No wonder if we're grateful, but feel measured
by the few who love once and stay married,
and who seem, after all this time and children,
still to like each other and to be decent,
in the small symptomatic signs, such as
not interrupting or correcting or turning on
against each other, who, as Frost says,
"Know too much and are not disinterested."

And of those we have thought thus lucky
how many split anyway, after 25 or 30 years,
finding love at last too hard to bear.
You remember when your own marriage
after 12 hard years was uncoiling,
how bitterly cynical you were,
devising for drinking friends the new marriage
in the new life after, perhaps, the revolution:
when marriages would last, by law, 5 years,
no more, unless couples applied for another 5—
the red tape as complicated as for divorce—
no children permitted till the second 5,
with those from unions that fail anyway

8

to be reared in something like the kibbutz,
away from failed love's poisons.

How did you manage to make this funny?
so that even your wife laughed—
though ruefully, through cuts and prophecy.

Of course you understand: these two you met may
have come to the unprecedented loneliness,
in distances between them of that little house—
made longer by the beautiful small children—
of love gone far away. Without it,
how could they go on with the rest of
what had made them beautiful together there.

You'd hope they'd never get their fill.
but you have no doubts they could, and did,
that they found, yes, enough of it, and bend.

Park River, North Dakota: 1939

"Pitch-black—and blood all over the alley,"
is how it reached you, 5 years old,
when the Mexicans killed each other
that Saturday night in Park River.

They used knives, being Mexican,
long ones, razor-sharp, and were drunk
also, and for the same reason,
having followed the harvest north.

You were afraid of anything Mexican
for a long time, afraid for your father,
who left on Saturday nights without
mother, who said we love Mexicans too.

And what was it later, in the Marines,
pulling weekends to Tijuana?—only whores
and beer? or a smell of blood, the lure of alleys,
and star-holes stuck in the body's night.

Juggle

This delicious skulduggery,
as one master calls it, requires

that you be perfectly normal with
"the Mrs.," but not too normal,
chatting of this or that.
                        To be
solicitous, but no more than usual,
flattering only if it comes easily:

to be a successful philanderer, first,
by being a perfect husband, that kind.

To telephone regularly, daily,
so you may triangulate to know
exactly where she is or will be,
when you are covert or sunk.

To be amorous, especially before and
after, but, again, within bounds.

To be ordinarily busy about the house
or yard or career or exercise,
and *errands*, yes many, as always.

To whistle innocence tunelessly, or
to be irritable, suddenly, over little,
if these are your faithful foils.

                        In short,
to keep the quotidian squashy
but honor the crucial routines.

Don't be surprised how long
you can keep them up—soon

11

yourself, a maestro of skulls
and dugs, of juggling and jugs.

Battle of the Bulge, 1944

Uncle Wilbur face down
for thirty hours in the mud,
his back broken, his spine shrapneled open,
the cord going off, off, in the fog.
By the time they find him,
the second morning, there is no pain,
and he is in a kind of dream,
on that strange bed but home,
someone gentle lifting him,
composing to straighten the changed legs
and rub his dead back warm all over,
in the misting rain of Belgium:
the war's whole diesel scat and drum,
from the heart down, front and back,
deaf dumb and paralyzed.

Nocturne

First he hears it under water,
the submarine taking direct hits or colliding—
or what's the sound? is it really springs?
Pitched high, muted little by distance,
the shanking stresses like a
metallic or electric hee-haw.
When he hears for sure, awake,
though he's never heard it before,
he knows at once: his parents making love.
He's 14 or 15, his father 44 or 45,
his mother a year younger,
and now, when he remembers it,
he's older than they all were—50.
Still, as he thought then, it took
an awfully long time for them to finish,
even stopping for what may have been a rest
before, it seemed to him grimly, going on.
There were tunneling deep coughs from his father,
some talking sounds from both, during the rest,
but silence, the long room away, silence otherwise
from both. Maybe it sounded a heavy chore to him
(if 14 still a virgin, if 15 maybe not),
and he felt sorry especially for his mother,
who seemed to be receiving love's version
of a methodically thorough beating all
the way through to some predetermined point
he and his siblings knew almost by heart.
Now he thinks the father punished as he did
to scourge by hand, razor-strap and fire-shovel
any persisting murder in the blood,
that maybe it also pounded in their love.
Then the boy lay there awake, eyes open to hear,
trying to be grown-up, trying to be amused,
thinking of telling his friends how funny,
but compromised to his bowels—orphaned in his digits.
He couldn't sleep he'd thought for a long time,
and his father was gone to work when he wakened.

14

He was angry with his mother's morning honey,
and embarrassed—ashamed—when she sang.
After 55 years of a life together,
his mother died at 78, leaving his father 79,
but now in his night as he thinks of them in theirs,
they are his juniors in their tasking.
Caught young in their mistakes and obligations,
and then after a year and the baby,
married again by two deaths that seared the families'
flesh, suicide cauterizing murder: their fathers.
Having lived 20 years in the nightmare scar
and bringing 5 more children to it,
on this night they try the dark again,
their odd son become a light sleeper who wakes
always—as perhaps everyone does?—by hearing.
There is much more to the story
and the fathers (especially) and sons
have much in the flesh to answer for.
But now these two seem in that long-ago dark
brave and sweet in their old restatement
of a contract to pry the murderous fathers'
hands from them, or a patient hard try to accept
again whatever love could not forgive,
of the night, the fathers, each other, even
the morbid boy, vexed in his dark past listening.

Measures

Late September, Early Morning

It's fall but he's written his fall poems,
his harvest poems and here comes age poems.
Few have noticed, but he's tried everything,
including birth life and death poems,
the dying Christ, the death of God,
the ministry of work poems, the insouciance
especially, Ivan Spornitz's, Bunk McVane's,
his father, grandmother Rose and others.
Himself he's covered like a wall, poster-full.
He's even tried Alaska and Korea,
Bulgaria and Iwo Jima (no visit required).
So now he's trying to wait, "patient to strike,"
under his peculiar illusion and weed it counts.
But something stubborn wants him scribbling daily,
even if *it* is the only thing to write about.
Like straw blown through a tree, it's in him,
or gratitude, to get up before dawn,
to sit at the cricketing window a while,
letting it in, and then to put it down here. And
after seeing his old friend madly flogging his book,
months now atop the *Times* best-seller list,
he's trying to work up a solace
that his obscurity, like this early morning's
dark, is the perfect light to work in.

Park River Valentines

Behind Skjervens' Garage and Dodge place,
in a lot cluttered with wrecks
we found an empty tank from,
we guessed, an old gas truck:
that's what its fumes said, addictively sweet.
I guess it was Tim Vavrosky's idea
for all of us, Turk, Tim, Shadow, and me,
to get into it, one at a time. Then
the rest would close the lids, like milk-can tops,
and with the rag-ends from Detroit—
exhaust-pipes, broken bumpers, hubcaps—
we'd culled out of piles behind the garage,
we banged and banged on the tank,
timing it, to see how long it was
before the clang-battered victim pushed
up the lid, and jacked himself out.
As in all the cruel tests of manliness,
there was a principal victim,
this time Shadow (so called because
too thin to cast one) who was elected,
probably by Tim, no meaner or more stupid
than we were but the oldest and the day's chief.
Us he instructed to plug our ears and yell
when each of us in turn was in the tank—and it worked.
The simple strategy to victimize lay in not
so advising Shadow, who had the finest ear,
therefore most abusable: even so,
it *was* awful and our ears rang too.
I guess he took our yelling and laughing,
as he was supposed to, as *our* not being the sissy.
And we won, because he cried in frustrated rage,
furiously banging and banging on the tank,
each of us in turn, and, finally, all of us inside,
yelling, taunting, holding our ears and singing,
as Shadow banged, over and over and over,

Up your ass and down my spine
Won't you be my Valentine?

Loud enough, in the ambivalent dark of our circle,
to deafen the gas-tank clamor
and ring the junkyard victory.

Measure for Elizabeth

I don't gauge the light perfection
until I see the small maple,
slender, full-leafed in its yellows,
up against the taller evergreens.

The slanting Indian summer seems
lofted by late afternoon just
over their tops to light this tree—

its buff transparencies fragile
to airiness, as if so near the edge
of every leaf's releasing
a chill would let them down at once.

It is deciduous from the Latin
verb to fall, and here before
it joins an ancient language
it is oriental grace and feminine
with delicate sashay, leaning or moving to
the permanent greens of measure.

Yes, slender and just emerging
in her name, one arm before
her, one hand up to hold
the pine needle branch away
as she takes quick small steps to enter.

Metrical Crystals or Snow

When love goes sorrow enters:
if physical loneliness were sound,
a water of far cars and crickets seeking
any body's place the probing tenders.

There are other symptoms,
a certain clogging here and,
especially, there.

                    But the first sign
is a homesick throat or Sunday chest,
from his lies or her suspicion: who knows
which acid eating through—as it were snow—
tungsten or cobalt or steel or the heart.

With Sharp Voices
(from WCW; for E)

There are 15 or 20 sparrows in the backyard
and 2 which may be grackles. I look it up:
yes—grackles, "black with metallic hues . . ."
but are they also "iridescent in the sunlight"?

Hard to tell, as there is little sun today,
yet the primary and secondary feathers are
certainly speckled, as might take a shine,
and the sun comes out, briefly, and they do.

The testy sparrows are, plainly, sparrows,
pecking those things that interest them.
I can't tell what does, though I watch them
for some time, pecking at *them* in a way—

maybe it is the coming rain to soak 2 days
and nights, keeping them in their nests
with no more food than they fill on here—
but now the rain is starting and they're gone.

Still

Today's paper carries this headline:
"Fading Taste for Bourbon Pinches Kentucky."
But a distiller named Bill Samuels, Jr.
is not concerned, saying the market
has always had its highs and lows, and besides,
he says, though his is a small company
with sales of only 125,000 cases a year,
he's doing fine: "We sell out of whiskey
every year, and you can hardly beat that
when everybody's wringing their hands."

His own brand is Maker's Mark,
his "Family has made whiskey for four
generations near Bardstown," Kentucky
and he tells the family story:
how an ancestor was mustered out of
the Revolutionary War in 1793,
moved to Kentucky, and turned to whiskey.
Land was offered to anyone who would settle,
raise corn, and stay 3 years. "This,"
says Samuels, "was most attractive to people
who knew what to do with corn . . .
they started making whiskey
and that was the first money of the west."
This story in the Lynchburg *News*
soaks in a high-mash flavor, which just
hints that if our taste is fading
it's because our tongues and palates
have been bleached by pacific chablis,
dulled by low-cal reds
and washed out by bad lite beer.

While "pinches Kentucky" gauges a slack
in the belly of the country's swagger,
as still hands are laid off
and recession more than taste trickles dry
down the mean alembics of the time.

25

Next the expert American of Mr Samuels,
whose border drawl is 200 years
into the hickory-tough grain of his saying
"We sell out of whiskey," and whose
work has had no trouble paying off
his father's his and his son's bills.
And so he understands the problem
to be one of quality-control,
or, as we used to say, know-how:
if all these poor hand-wringing
sons of whiskey-makers only
knew what to do with that corn . . . ,
an oak-aged 100-proof canticle
of knowing what to do with the hands.
And what about *Bards*town?
Was this whiskey town named for a poet?
Or all poets?—I doubt it—
probably for some John or Henry or Bill Bard.
But this American Samuels and Samuels' son
has made his name with Maker's Mark, a bourbon
bearing the poet's verb (*poiein*) to make:
as if from the secret empty spaces
in that seed kernel of corn
planted in a dark and bloody ground
by revolutionary regulars, we make
not only the feed to tame wild turkeys
and the first hard coin of
our brusquely scalawagging west,
but refine as well, from the corn's raw dream,
a forked white-lightning, home-brewed
or the straight and sour-mash lyric of our genius
that everclear or red jagging water
river branch and grain
we drink our history in.

Snug Harbor, New Orleans

The "Soprano Saxophone Shootout" at Snug Harbor,
outside the quarter in New Orleans, was stone
improvisation for 3 sets by black Earl, the boss,
young black Victor, and Tony, white and young.

They were backed up all night by two white players,
the drummer Vidacovich and one Singleton on bass.
I liked the plain cat-friendliness that came,
slowly, quiet with the playing—for excellence.

I liked being in a real jazz joint, in New Orleans,
grateful to the Bucharest Cajun who sent me there,
far from the Bourbon St. dives charging 6 bucks a pop,
where only money and booze have jazzed for years.

I liked how the white guy Tony held his own,
less hot, though, and more bookish, whiter,
in the free-fall wail, how at ease, cross color,
all 5 were—musicians—more and more as the night.

I was moved by the riffs, the sonorous blare,
the brand new Bach and Thelonious harmonies,
the way they played more things together
as if they were finding something slowly: it.

I improvised too, switching drinks—vodka,
Jack Daniels (a burger) some Rum-Monsoons—
till 3 A.M., then back to the hotel to sleep 4 hours
and wake clear as a stone booze-rinsed in a song.

Two weeks later, at 4:30, I'm up to say I can
still hear those saxes getting down, and wish
I were Al Young or Matthews or Zimmer, to sing it
mournful and joyous, joyful and mourning and gone.

Gift

Now here is a poem for Nancy
who, along with Mark,
let me read her my brand new
bourbon whiskey poem.
Not only because she let me
and agreed to my rules beforehand—
that they must like it, say so, and mean it—
and not only because when I'd read it
she liked it and meant it
but also and overridingly,
may the mystery bless her,
because she said, wait,
first I'm going to lie down.
We were in Mark's studio
and she lay down on the couch,
closing her eyes,
the better to welcome my whiskey poem.

Without ever knowing it,
all my obscure scribbler's life
I have wanted to write one poem
a woman beautiful as Nancy
would want, like that, to lie down for.
I thank her for revealing this,
for liking my poem about whiskey
and for meaning it,
but most for lying down.

When I go to the writer's last place
I will say for credentials,
I am Flint: I wrote one poem
Nancy the muse lay down for.

Stubborn

To persever
In obstinat condolement is a course
Of impious stubbornness; 'tis unmanly grief:
It shows a will most incorrect to heaven;
A heart unfortified, a mind impatient.

Hamlet

Stubborn

On a rainy Sunday I have an optional meeting
with my students, and eleven show up.
We have a good time talking ninety minutes or so
about James Wright's "To a Blossoming Pear Tree."
Afterwards, though I had thought to stay in my office,
I decide to go home, because I'm too agitated to work,
having drunk a large cup of strong coffee
instead of my usual decaffeinated stuff.
I call Rosalind to tell her I'm coming home,
and she seems glad but, as she had earlier this morning,
also a bit depressed. Why? She thinks it's because,
although she's happy to be going back to New Zealand,
    tomorrow,
she's sad about leaving her sons and me at Christmas.
So I decide to get her some flowers on the way home.

I buy a bunch each of blue and white irises
and three yellow sweetheart roses.
At the busy florist's there is a woman of 27 or 28
wearing a sweatshirt with my school's name on it.
I don't know her, but she glances as if she recognizes me.
She has thick blond hair with some soft reds in it,
and I think it is not so red or fine as my son's hair was.
I also think she looks some like the daisies she's picking out.
And I think to put in a poem some time
a woman's hair with the colors of a daisy's eye.

Driving home I come aware how beautifully
iris folds in and out upon itself,
like someone in grief, like my mother in hers,
her long sad life, which ended seventy-seven days ago.
It occurs to me, though I had told the clerk no ferns
(because they remind me of funeral sprays)
that when she absently asked me again if I wanted ferns,
I said yes, as absently, which makes me realize
how much my mother is on my mind, buried
on the eleventh anniversary of the boy's death.

Also, not quite refusing it but resisting it,
I can't keep out the solace: he is with her now.
And even as I'm annoyed to suppose
I'll put this too in a poem some time,
I think of the boy's mother, of my mother, my wife,
these women in their sorrows, and consider
some failures touching all of them,
the irises and roses beside me on the seat.

On Nebraska Avenue I see a very small boy
walking on the grass between the sidewalk and the street,
alone except for a big golden retriever, near him.
I can't tell if they are together. When it comes to me
the boy really is alone, so near the street, and only two years
    old,
or younger, my stomach moves, with fear.
I pull over, stop the car, get out and ask a jogger,
who is slowing to a walk, if he knows the boy. No, he
    doesn't.
I try to be calm and talk quietly to the boy.
Where do you live? where is *your* house?
He doesn't answer, the cars blowing by, but
seems to wave toward the dog. I say let's go there,
and try to smile him into walking along with me,
aware the jogger has stopped and, as I would do,
is wondering about me and what I might be up to.
I don't try to take the boy's hand. Mine, I see, is trembling.
He doesn't speak: he may not be old enough to speak.

Then I hear someone scared and calling—we're next to
a steeply banked yard, behind a wall, chest-high.
I see the parents running down, and hear them calling a
    name.
I pick up the boy under his arms slowly as I can,
and hold him up so they can see him. He does not cry out.
The mother is nodding, yes, and waves relief. They are not
coming from the direction I was trying to get the boy to go.

I put him down and now he takes my hand as we walk,
back around the corner, toward his parents.
When he sees his father, he pulls away, and, making wordless
   noises,
runs to him, back onto the grass, next to the curb.
The father is so angry with himself
he begins yelling: "*Michael, where did you* go?"
and I say, too loudly, hearing how my voice is shaking,
"I think he's very frightened now," hoping
he will stop yelling at his son—and he does stop.
Michael wants his father to come with him,
back to the corner, where he points at the dog.
"Ah," says his father, and calls to him: "*Bennie!*"
Bennie comes running. Michael had been following Bennie.

We talk, they thank me, they had just now noticed
Michael somehow got out in the rain.
As the guilty father talks me back to my car,
I answer carefully, trying to hold my voice down.
I tell him *I understand,* that my oldest daughter
somehow got out when she was eighteen months
and almost got into the street, how a neighbor
took her in and called me. *I understand.*
I don't want to say more, and I'm afraid I'll start crying,
but I have to, to make it clearer:
I tell him my son was killed in the street like this.
He says "Really?" and thanks me again, and I leave.

I don't start crying until I get back in the car—
and I'm furious and groan with it to know,
even then, in spite of myself, that I'll write about this
as well, pulled through the pages by something,
as if in the hand, to write it down here.
Besides despair of writing it well enough
is this revulsion at smearing grief
in order to do it, to use a poem as if you were
trading what you have lived through for *words,*

selling out, by using, the worst secrets.
But the words come anyway. So when, finally,
I have to write them down, I fear
I may be stupidly tempting death, and yet
I write them as if my life is the poem to give—
its work come clearly, saying, go and write,
do what has been given to do, and
if it is given in grief accept it there,
where you may see whatever else is given:
this time Michael following Bennie in the rain
has made you feel in his small hand bones
the unknown body of his living,
his unrepeatable life, which you write down
as if it were your own, as if this
prayer Michael might have his life
is something mending yours. And maybe it is.

Certain Slants

A Certain Slant

Washington sits in a vellum light, or buff,
some evenings, after the cherry blossoms,
after forsythia, before azaleas bank and flare:
a light as if for painters, which lets you see
clear definition of the black slates and numbers
on a Georgetown steeple-tower and clock,
even from a block or two away, as now.

                          And here,
as if light's foil, a student in blindfold
is led across the lawns by two young women,
who turn him and caution and guide him,
to a small dogwood—under a branch of which
they must depress his head and shoulders
to get him past.

               All three are laughing
with the innocent charade of fatal
tangles, forgetful mazes, open wells,
the perils there they save him from,
orphan or hostage to the game.

                    They clear
the low-bridge of this branch, and
its pinked white petals
filter sun-light, trembling,
as it's bumped and left behind.

The captive one steps boyishly confused
at being touched and led by two:
blind master of a wise compliance, chatty
and helpless in their hands, as if
he is one the vellum bears—and is—
the twilight rising where they go.

Cinema

She is talented, pretty, myopic,
has round perfect breasts
and in three days makes love
with four men she didn't want:
like a dream she says,
as if she lay there watching.

She always enters smiling,
trying to see everyone,
bumping this and bumping that,
wanting to hold things and
bring them close enough to see—closer.

(Can eyes like other organs of receipt
come to their time and bleed
in sympathy of some abuse?—
hers do, spontaneously.)

The lovers: the first unpacks her,
spotting a fear of strangers.
The second touches her
with songs about poor vision.
The third is British:
brilliant, campy and hard,
whose kindness when he comes
is irresistible, somehow
as if the BBC should whisper love
or Oxford shill for her pictures.

She's working on a series of drawings,
a sort of movies' progress each by each
of another, younger, man.
He is naked
with straight long Navajo hair,
a body poorly or indistinctly muscled,
with a face stretched flat between big ears.

In the first frame
he's holding a peach-basket
upside down above his head:
he looks up into it as if it's looking back,
holding the wire handles on the sides.

As the series goes on,
the light-wood sides of the basket
seem to bevel and splay,
like moist wide tobacco leaves opening,
as, frame by frame,
he lowers it over his forehead,
then his eyes, and then down over his chin.

At last the head is gone, when he
enters her basket or leaves his face
and the picture is complete.

Ng Ga Pe or Ng Gar Pay, a Digest
—November 7, 1984, for CS

These were two small fiery drinks,
spelled both ways, rice whiskey
with a sweet taste behind the 90 proof or so,
along with the BoBo Platter for Two,
I shared with the visiting poet.

We had talked about Sofia, Belgrade,
our trips there, as well as Kuwait,
Holland and China, other places
we'd been to or wanted to see.
At lunch I'd had Eggs Benedict,
hard as a sorcerer's eyeballs,
and he an overdone chopped steak
with the salty Bloody Marys.

After his reading we had
California wine with the students
and then rowan-flavored Polish vodka
with my friends, a Russian Jew, an Irish Catholic
and the Slovak priest from Classics.

Over the BoBo Platter
we compared Bulgarian and Yugoslavian dishes
and I told him two nights before
how my daughter and I had
had the Greek bean soup in one place
French-fried onions at another
and main courses *Chez Vietnam.*

So it had an American rightness
the brainless day after Reagan's sweep
for a mixed Celt (me) and the Yankee Serb—
grousing about their parents' votes—
to have two strong Ng Ga Pes
and the BoBo Platter before
he went for his interview with the mad Italian

and I came home to write this down
and eat a little Kiwi fruit.

Sonnet in a Square Vase

Upon the table, before his earnest gaze,
the little bulbs of the squared-up daffodils
are fading slowly, almost blinking out,
the lower petals peeling off, aghast,
seared triangular lampshades, pinked back.
Yet each blossom's bulb or mouth or trumpet
still is shining or saying or wailing
something he almost hears, the tongues erect,
a little green still leaching in the throat.
Are they whispering good-bye green-yellow song,
or sending in all directions, to forsythias,
to spring or crocus, just hello, good-bye?
Wait: what someone has brought home
to change the dinner, lighting asparagus
like lemon, is telling a spring morning
what the four corners of his day should be.

A Divorce

These days like sex the trouble is
they want it at different times:
he wants it at night when she feels empty,
she wants it in the morning when he wakes full.
One needs to sleep or stay awake a shift
to get their split in gear,
because, like the divorce these days
even sex their diamond is
sharply fogging up on them,
as one morning when
(instead of love) she turns
over to face him bearing down
upon her elbow to tell him
her bad dream: how
they'd moved to a high new house,
he, she, her kids, his, *but*
it turned out to be the old house yet—
add mice and rats and cinders,
slow sinking floors and stairs—
and he was, she says,
telling her that her stomach hurts,
he kept on saying so and she kept asking
why are you telling me this? *Why?*
Was the new house their love formerly?
the old one what it's come to?
Surely the stomachache is how he bullies,
always telling her what she feels,
also the baby they didn't have together
or the operation to prevent it accuses,
or else he's telling her, empty,
I know you've had a bellyful of me
or he's blaming the whole on her
when really both want out as well
as in. Both cheaters somehow, if
one more than the other, but
both in a Mary McCarthy sentence once:

43

The betrayer is always the debtor;
at best he can only work out in remorse
his deficit of love, until remorse itself
becomes love's humble shame-faced proxy.

Too clever, of course, if true,
to say their sorries, yeah me too.

Bang!

When I was splitting the wood with
agreeable violence and accuracy, settled
into full-arc swings of the sledge, bang
on the long blue wedge, bang upon the red,

splitting the big trunk rounds of maple
into lengths little thicker than kindling,
my neighbor offered, over the fence,
that I was "doing that with a vengeance."

Maybe, partly, and why not? if I can
still swing it so, at 52, as, probably,
I won't be able to in 10 years, even 5,
Bang! few pauses, Bang! all afternoon.

Well, vengeance on what?—How about
death and aging and marriage and flesh
and grief and writing and money and death:
bottomless pits, pitiless bottoms.

But *mostly* just to accept, to a steady beat,
the gifts of timing and strength and
precision: Bang!-swing it-Bang!-swing it-
Bang! Goddamned hard. All afternoon.

Rosemary

How recollection fills with blood
to bring you back from thirty years,
briary blonde of head and thighs
as delicate as my lobeless ears,

you said, were not. Remember that?
You said they were a comic-opera size,
that it would take a head as big as mine
to finesse my smaller nose and eyes.

And what have we become—in 1989?
If I'm fifty-five you're fifty-three!
But memory still fixes your
small hands and avid mouth on me.

When, span by span, you gauged my head,
I thought neither of us would stray—
but both did—many lives ago one night,
like any whom the nights betray.

So just give thanks, when they come back,
if only so, those evenings where we held
with all who think time's wheeling slows,
as memory and need and senses meld.

A Spotted Cat in Indonesia

Black and white, it is climbing slates
of a roof below my window, in Surabaya,

a thin *Felis catus,* in a loping clamber
to the peak, where it sits and looks about.

I thought it was chasing something, some
cat thing in its mind or eye to do—sun

and shade mixing under trees on the slates—
something to eat, or go after for play.

But before it goes down the other side, out
of view, it stops, and seems to be taking stock.

Not of me—it hasn't spotted me watching
how the roof's pitch makes its climbing bob,

any more than it knows the *International Tribune*
for today reports hundreds of cats found mummified

in Aper-El's tomb, in Egypt, near the temple
of Bastet, cat goddess and protectress of

the hearth, maybe of peaks and slates hereafter.
What and how it *does* see or know, in its way,

of the birds, morning, death, or shade, Indonesia,
or what its life is to it any morning on the roofs,

who knows? maybe a pleasant dream, repeating,
everything only half familiar, uninfluenced

by precedent, unweary of choosing this and that
forever, even its running uphill something slated

outside itself or in its legs in their going.
And while calmly doing what its morning is,

before this up and down, where was I? Scratching
about the journey, carefully repacking for customs,

going down for spiky odd fruit and the paper,
reading in the lobby, worrying connections—

Malang, Surabaya, Jakarta, Singapore, London,
home. And, just now, as I paused for the cat,

though vague on exactly why I was invited here,
and utterly lost a block away in any direction,

I was fussing over whether the hotel laundry
has mislaid which socks, and how to complain or not.

Anniversaries

They ceased not from their own doings,
nor from their stubborn way.

What Forgiveness

Last week on a street in Washington,
I saw two dark women, who looked like sisters,
but who may have been mother and daughter,
forty-two and twenty-four.

I don't know if they actually looked Iranian
or if it was that the younger woman's arms
had been chopped off, one above, one
below the elbow, roughly, it looked
from the scarred and jagged stumps, as
a while ago, before Khomeini, we heard
was sometimes done to the Shah's enemies'
children, the dying fathers forced
to watch, a plain example.

As it must have been with the fathers,
so it was impossible for me to look
or not to look, so that now
if I can't quite see them on the air,
I can't blink them away either, all of it,
the older woman a step or two ahead,
both walking fast, the second
hard-eyed and merciless, furiously
short-sleeved, pumping as if to
swing what is left of her bare arms.

This morning I wake thinking of her,
again, her picture stinging the air
like my glancing away, with something like
panic at many details of what she cannot
do for herself—
                    the woman with her,
maybe always with her, everywhere
with her, tying and fixing and
buttoning, changing and touching
and cleaning this and that and that—

51

I wake with revulsion and fury against
the butcher and his Shah, to think what
the small child knew—and bears,
and with the usual helplessness at what
my country was and is to theirs,
with or without the Shah.

Yes, and with sorrow for the Shah,
if the charge is false, even some
for his soul on that spit, if it's true.

But it is the child's face I never saw,
persisting, maybe because of
the television rebroadcasts, now,
the anniversary of the floods and landslides
in Colombia, of that small girl, her
legs crushed, trapped in the mud—
two days of confused smiling at the fatal
camera, blowing kisses, waiting to be saved.

(How could they not get her out,
for Christ's sake, in *two days*?
could *anyone* have done it?)

Officially, she died of a heart attack,
but of course she died of being cold,
wet and, especially, young
and unable to move for two days.
And her face becomes the Iranian girl's,
as if the buried child could survive
to hurtle down the street like this,
a rage for never letting go—
of the Shah, his butcher, us.

And the butcher? who held her small-boned
arms in his hand, one at a time, the knife
in the other, her little struggle nothing,

her screaming, or her father's, ecstatic carving
along his blood: surely he's dead, we hope
no one human could live with that blade
stuck up under his ribs and brain.

But we know very well he may be
a traffic cop in Beirut or Cairo, waving,
a whitely wielded baton for the TV news,
or the man who fixes your Plymouth
in Virginia, who is childishly proud
of his English, who shows you snapshots
of his wife and children, who gives you
a good deal, whose buried memory of
that moment may be the secret lining
his heart, of satin, of silk brocade.

Anniversaries

How cruel a dream can be
you find out when you watch
a surviving daughter dying
and dead in place of the boy,
both injured, but the boy making his way,
alive, and you discover with others
how she had made a birthday cake,
frosted it a glossy black,
upon which several had signed
their names in sugar white.
Witnesses to prophecy?
It's not clear. But
she had foreseen it all.

What punishments do you deeply
prescribe yourself to dream
this guilty retrospective
of history too horrid to revise?
and revise in such poisoning detail
that in it she says "Daddy" and "Good-bye,"
your whole chest clotted, broken—
it's clear in the dream—
the way his was.

When you finally waken you know
this was no dream of preference
but rage at losing forever, refusal
fighting refusal—and non-negotiable fact:
a crushed chest the literal broken
heart and long wish you'd died instead,
all tormented starving for the boy,
aware how death, if it dealt, would deal.

Jim

I gave my lunch apple to a horse
yesterday and remembered the horse,
who was your "friend David,"
eating the only copy of one poem
in Minnesota. So last night
I reread your final book again,
moving among the Ohio, French,
and especially Italian people and animals
of your last journey.

Some of the resolved gentleness here
makes me cry, your welcoming
of the blue spider not so much as
this late acceptance of the self.

I was often moved when you wrote
of your preferring lions in His name,
"Small wonder Jesus wept at a human city."

But I am more moved now when you
make me believe the turtle
to be a man of God, with its
"Religious face," meaning unswervably
perfect to itself, I guess, to you,
perfect to me in your language.

Holding the book, I read,
watching your father and the fat Ohioans
tremble in my hands.

I close it at last, and
looking at the jacket-back
I bid the picture and your name goodnight.

Then in the dark I try
to sleep right through the
stone beasts ghosts and angels

55

of my stubborn grief who bear
Ohio after Fano.

Pamela, on February 8, 1982

My daughter is sweet sixteen today,
and this is not just a thing to say,
because she is that dearer sweetness
steeped in grief: for her brother
dead almost ten years now,
twin and darling of her sixth year's heart.
And she bears him with her still
on her birthday, feeling as I do
how old the boy is too this year:
wondering hopelessly what would be.
I could wish her birthdays free of this,
but how can they be? "The boy is dead,"
the doctor's sentence permanent.
To wish her uncomplicated happy birthdays
would be to wish the boy alive or out of thought,
one as impossible as the other.
So she is early knowing what
every human love is soaked in.
We will have our quiet celebration,
her choice of menu, a fire to watch,
some useful presents and some not,
and some time in the day
she will find me alone
and speak to me of her brother.
We'll hold each other
and then go on, the boy between us,
an obligation on our love
to live for him as well: *Ethan.*

What I Have Tried to Say to You

That there are ways to love the life you haven't had,
ways to forgive the one you have.
That while your brother wasn't killed
to test anyone, his death is,
somehow, allowed by the mystery
requiring our lives to have this
permanent pull at the middle.
Our lives are what they have been: unrevisable,
changed only in our responses,
if we are still ready, somehow,
for the next day, the next
person, poem, chance, even prepared,
however unready, for the next death.
Can we permanently grieve the boy
without hating what has become of him?
What *has* become of him?
He has returned to mystery,
the same one that is our life,
mine and yours this morning,
the continuing shapes we never see
up there, this afternoon, tomorrow:
so he is already, ahead of time,
in everything we do. I feel it, often,
that I am living my life in part for him,
not permanently dead in us, but telling
how we'd rather he had lived than not.
Remember our game of listening in the park
to hear the woods fill up with sounds,
birds, mostly, from farther and farther away
the longer we listened. He seems now
especially to have listened,
raptly, eyes closed, as if to singing,
as if he were entering the song,
and like the way he usually walked
far ahead of us or far behind—
already gone to his own music.
When I think how long it is

since he has entered all silence,
it takes me by the heart to think
those sounds like light have stayed
in whatever we are left to be.
That songs we heard those days
are from the place he's gone away to,
a singing in the mysteries connecting us,
if we can stop and be quiet and listen.

Black Sea, Mother and Son

This woman of thirty-two or -three,
her dark hair shining,
has brought herself and her
child of two-and-a-half or three
into the early morning sun
of a June day near the Black Sea
coast.
    When the mother
glances up from the child's face,
she can see the darkening water
from here—
        over the tops of densely
tufted pear and thickly bearing
cherry trees,
        over the head of an old man,
who moves in stately half-step
cutting grass very short with
precise repeated swings
of his scythe,
        over weedless gardens of irises,
peonies, daisies and roses,
whose rough-mixed scents
accompany birds that have been
singing the sky full:
            earlier,
the song of nightingales,
but mostly, now,
a throaty treble of swallows.

Because it is June,
when poplars winnow the
blue skies ragged they yield
a snowy summer cotton,
which women have been
sweeping up since dawn
before rinsing the
terrace stones,

so
vacationers at white tables
may take the sun with tea,
like cheese with bread,
while looking up to receive
as well the odd comfort
of a flying sea.

And here the mother has
been charming her son to eat
his cupful of milk and bread
and honey, while she drinks the
sweet black Turkish coffee she loves.
The boy is beautiful
because he is young,
but also bright and
healthy and with his mother,
who is beautiful for similar
reasons,
            and, though settled
in this calm of a holiday's
repose, she is also avid,
some light from in her
giving back the old southern
sun as if she were beginning
a morning summers and summers
ago in Sicily or Greece or
Mesopotamia,
                hung with olive and
lemon and pepper and grape
and blood orange,
                but it is
an ordinary hillside
on the Balkan peninsula,
north of Varna and south of
Zlatni Pyasetsi,
as it was a thousand
years ago or yesterday.

Sicily

Sicily

After rereading John Cheever for months,
you consider, on this island which perfects his view,
that, though his many rains approve
"the harsh surface beauty of life,"
he finds earth's humans to be bewildered,
which seems to mean not merely that life is confusing,
but that it is both absorbing and dull, pained and sweet,
addictive and merciless—vexed, like laughter in grief.

Because of an invitation that came
three days before you would set out,
you find yourself in Sicily, in Nicosia—
where the rain has been falling to soften,
all night, the harsh and beautiful hills—
which you have traveled to from Washington,
then from Rome, Catania and Acireale,
and the quick decision and changes
have left you bewildered yourself.

Nicosia is a city on top of a small mountain,
where you are in a hotel with every shining amenity,
much pale carnelian marble, hotly buffed,
but surrounded, on slopes pitching down, by jagged and
    torn
Sicilian rocks, engrained and pocked—from time and
    sirocco—
with history's grime, looking like what peppers
the Trevi Fountain's travertine marble, in Rome.

You are in a small party of writers, feted and pampered
by these Sicilians, their noisy wines, big rough breads,
exacting pastas and manner, chewy with history.
Every taste that focuses and winds a foreign
palate, blood orange to lemon pepper,
seems both raucous and subtle, Sicilian,
like the polite but fuming pastor

urging his poets upon you—Ganci,
Grasso, and homegrown Pirandello.

As thrusting up through everything—
like rocks in the marble lobby or
hung totems of garlic and clove,
like gargoyles cut in the altar—
are invisible hints of the shotgun
and a prohibition of women you feel at once.

One night, half asleep or dreaming,
you hear crystal splintering thinly as stars,
and some furious male shouting, which recalls
bandy Polyphemo, in different souvenir sizes,
as if he were flinging the hoisted boulders
blind through the gift-shop window.
Last night, in front of a hundred Nicosians,
you sat with Swedes, Bulgarians and Russians,
to speak and read some words, which were then translated.
Near the front, raptly staring, was a girl of seven or so:
if any adult and adult occasion is bewildering to a child,
what did she make of this jangle of poems and custom?
It occurred to you, as she followed the translations,
that she understood more in her way than you did,
while, in your way, you had another version.

Neither difference nor perception is unusual,
but of the harsh world's stranger puzzles,
what is rumbling Etna to people in
Catania, Nicolosi, Acireale, and other
cities in the permanent radius of risk?—
this cathedral of cloud and acrid snow,
which first exploded twenty-five hundred years ago,
to Aeschylus and Pindar, who wrote of it,
and which these Sicilians call Putana, whore,
because unpredictable, hot and open.

But in her lurid rivers of burning blood all night,
more like the secrets in dark stained glass—or Christ.

You see it first one night from the bus:
Antonio, the driver, tells what the seventeenth-century
eruptions filled or melted in his city,
what the earthquakes hit and missed,
then quietly sings, for those of you seated behind him,
a piece of the tenor's part from *Cavalleria Rusticana*.

You are driven on through the dark Sicilian night,
Etna, in view all the way, improvising news
from a jazzy center, and hotly forging belief,
you think, in those who see her all their lives.
True or not, you take it as scratching the puzzle,
at least, of such thoughts dusting a modest invention.

And if you don't quite trust it, so it comes:
that this serious young Catanian, Grazia Martinez—
a linguist who speaks a charming English,
though here to translate for the Russians—
because Etna has been out her window forever,
believes in Christ, her marriage, the future—
but not separate from molten grime and catastrophe.

Stranger, and making you warier:
Grazia reminds you of your mother. Before
coming to Nicosia, on a bright day in Acireale,
when one of the foreigners gives her a marzipan,
she says, "Thank you, yes, I must give you something too,"
and, offering with one hand, the brilliant shore,
standing in the sun herself, Spanish and Sicilian,
"I give you our sea at Acireale today—and the sky," she says,
lightly, and calm as your mother. Though your mother,
without Etna, had no such early promise to her life,
no belief for solace ever, except in children, whom,
one by one, she taught love's offices as gifts.

How bewildering that moments of her difficult life—
and its meaning, if any, beyond itself—insist to you,
through Grazia this morning in Sicily, as never
since her death. As, before she went to the hospital
for a simple knee surgery, not to return, your mother
hung, in deliberate prominence, two dresses in her closet,
others pushed right and left away, either of which,
she had told your sisters, would do one day for her burial.

Where did such fear or foreknowledge come from
in a woman who had survived much worse: besides
the hysterectomy were surgeries for gall bladder,
painful varicose veins, a burst vessel in her stomach,
and seven pregnancies in ten years—a miscarriage
and six children breaking the ground.

And how strange that in her last letter,
which reached you after the funeral, she wrote,
"I'm going to the hospital tomorrow.
I don't feel good about it."

In another, such gestures as the dresses
and letter might be a simple preventive magic,
but she had known too many sorrows to bargain—
tragedy as well: a family suicide and murder—
and she was not slight.

Something stops you to figure how long she has been dead:
you make it to be three years, three months,
and three days short of three weeks, bringing along
that she was buried, four days later,
on the anniversary of the child's death, yours:
making the worst season's worst addition.
So how can you account for its seeming proper now?—
as if a comfort, as if this symmetry of dates and numbers
were its own mystery to salve or line
the permanent crack in your chest.

Whatever secret of kindreds calling these to Sicily
also calls your sister, fifty-five, the tough one,
bossy as her father, but inconsolable because
her mother was put in the ground, as if death's body
were the end of love, scaring and confusing her grief:
"I can't stop thinking we just put her in the ground
and left her there."

And it's bewildering this morning
that what you've tried to shut out
for your daily life and work,
you are so grateful to be letting in
the return of grief is made suspicious,
as if invited, to sink in—as if to display.

Still you seem to believe in it, as if this too,
suspicion as self-knowing, were mysteriously
precious, and questions and dim awarenesses
do persist. As to you, in rainy Nicosia,
brooding through Cheever, his light
and liquid surfaces, the tangled core,
remembering and grieving with your siblings,
thinking of Grazia, Acireale, Antonio, Etna,
letting them in through worry and doubt,
trying their faulty or hidden connections,
attending your mother, son, and others in the ground,
whose afterlife, if any, poets say,
may be their times in our remembering.

Poetry from Illinois

History Is Your Own
Heartbeat
Michael S. Harper (1971)

The Foreclosure
Richard Emil Braun (1972)

The Scrawny Sonnets and
Other Narratives
Robert Bagg (1973)

The Creation Frame
Phyllis Thompson (1973)

To All Appearances: Poems
New and Selected
Josephine Miles (1974)

The Black Hawk Songs
Michael Borich (1975)

Nightmare Begins
Responsibility
Michael S. Harper (1975)

The Wichita Poems
Michael Van Walleghen (1975)

Images of Kin: New and
Selected Poems
Michael S. Harper (1977)

Poems of the Two Worlds
Frederick Morgan (1977)

Cumberland Station
Dave Smith (1977)

Tracking
Virginia R. Terris (1977)

Riversongs
Michael Anania (1978)

On Earth as It Is
Dan Masterson (1978)

Coming to Terms
Josephine Miles (1979)

Death Mother and Other
Poems
Frederick Morgan (1979)

Goshawk, Antelope
Dave Smith (1979)

Local Men
James Whitehead (1979)

Searching the Drowned Man
Sydney Lea (1980)

With Akhmatova at the Black
Gates
Stephen Berg (1981)

Dream Flights
Dave Smith (1981)

More Trouble with the
Obvious
Michael Van Walleghen (1981)

The American Book of the
Dead
Jim Barnes (1982)

The Floating Candles
Sydney Lea (1982)

Northbook
Frederick Morgan (1982)

Collected Poems, 1930-83
Josephine Miles (1983)

The River Painter
Emily Grosholz (1984)

Healing Song for the Inner
Ear
Michael S. Harper (1984)

The Passion of the Right-
Angled Man
T. R. Hummer (1984)

Dear John, Dear Coltrane
Michael S. Harper (1985)

Poems from the Sangamon
John Knoepfle (1985)

Eroding Witness
Nathaniel Mackey (1985)
National Poetry Series

In It
Stephen Berg (1986)

Palladium
Alice Fulton (1986)
National Poetry Series

The Ghosts of Who We Were
Phyllis Thompson (1986)

Moon in a Mason Jar
Robert Wrigley (1986)

Lower-Class Heresy
T. R. Hummer (1987)

Poems: New and Selected
Frederick Morgan (1987)

Cities in Motion
Sylvia Moss (1987)
National Poetry Series

Furnace Harbor: A
Rhapsody of the North
Country
Philip D. Church (1988)

The Hand of God and
a Few Bright Flowers
William Olsen (1988)
National Poetry Series

Bad Girl, with Hawk
Nance Van Winckel (1988)

Blue Tango
Michael Van Walleghen (1989)

The Great Bird of Love
Paul Zimmer (1989)
National Poetry Series

Eden
Dennis Schmitz (1989)

Waiting for Poppa at the
Smithtown Diner
Peter Serchuk (1990)

Great Blue
Brendan Galvin (1990)

Stubborn
Roland Flint (1990)
National Poetry Series